Living in the Shadow of Baldur's Death

Bryan Wilton

~ 1 ~

Contents

~ 3 ~

Preface

There are a lot of gaps in our lore. I believe it is that way for a reason. It is left to us to figure out how this material is going to help us grow. Recently I have been giving this quite a lot of thought. The series of books I have written have been a very cathartic event. Almost unaware of what was truly happening I have been shedding certain vestiges of ego and other, unseemly, characteristics of my being. When I became aware of what I was doing I took a little time and began to wonder about it. Why had I been doing this? Because I knew that buried within myself as well as within the lore there was deeper understanding to be had. I began to realize that my awareness at times was developing far past the surface material. I was hungrier than I had ever been to "see" something.   I kept catching glimpses of understanding in my dealings with people. I had written about the struggles of just about everything a man or woman may have to deal with in life. All of it has led to this work, the parallels that still exist between the struggles of the gods and the trials of being human. To think that these ancient high mythologies might still have a bearing upon us as individuals today is truly remarkable.

And yet we are not seeing the effects of a positive spiritual approach on the folk who follow Asatru. With such a long passing of time between these ages when our ancestors honored the gods with sacrifices and noble lives until now, it's no wonder. Gone are the men and women who truly understood the rites of initiation from boy and girl to men and women. The interpretation of the lore has been left to everyone and very, very few have been willing to make those sacrifices of personality necessary to grow in such a manner that we may assist the gods in their divine mission, whatever that may be. You see them take the easy way out with regards to how they apply the lore to building faith in their lives. Perhaps that is a part of the draw. We are as yet, a spiritually immature way of life. It's time to fix that.

Bryan Wilton   11 Jan 2015

The Mystery of Gullveig

We have all heard, at one point or another that Gullveig is Freya and we have most likely heard just as many people say she is not. Gullveig means "love of gold or gold lover" depending upon whom you ask. As for me, the idea that Freya, a positive example of prosperity and abundance, would be compared to Gullveig and the love of gold which is greed has never made sense. And almost as if to add insult to injury there is another being that is apparently totally unrelated that people will lump in with Freya as well. Freya is a master of Seidhr and gave instruction to

Odin himself, but this being is the flip side of that coin and is a joy to evil women. This, also, is out of line with what lore we have concerning Freya. But don't just take my word for it. I've done some research to provide justification of my idea. There are two names for the female beings which are referred to in these passages, but are they the same? The short answer is "No." Let's look to the Voluspa and see what it says.

21. The war I remember, | the first in the world,
When the gods with spears | had smitten Gollveig,
And in the hall | of Hor had burned her,

Three times burned, | and three times born,
Oft and again, | yet ever she lives.

22. Heith they named her | who sought their home,
The wide-seeing witch, | in magic wise;
Minds she bewitched | that were moved by her magic,
To evil women | a joy she was.

This passage seems to be very clear Gollveig was smitten and three times burned and three times reborn. But in the following passage gold doesn't appear to be a problem until three maids appear:

8. In their dwellings at peace | they played at tables,
Of gold no lack | did the gods then know,--
Till thither came | up giant-maids three,
Huge of might, | out of Jotunheim.

So when we open up with the Voluspa we are told that gold is not a problem, entire grand palaces of the gods are lined with it, then, enter stage left three giantesses appearing from Jotunheim. Some folk have argued that these are the Norns themselves, but they are not. They are the sinister infiltrating a golden age of Asgard when it was young and new. The Voluspa continues on to name the dwarves and then it circles back around and points out the nourishment required of Ygddrasil and then we see this:

20. Thence come the maidens | mighty in wisdom,
Three from the dwelling | down 'neath the tree;
Urth is one named, | Verthandi the next,--
On the wood they scored, -- | and Skuld the third.
Laws they made there, and life allotted
to the sons of men, and set their fates.

Maidens come, they bring balance back to the realms and they allot the lives of men. They came from the dwelling beneath the tree. They have originated from the power source of Yggdrasil itself. They come from the same place as the runes themselves, at the base of the tree. Consider this for just a moment. The appearance of something so vile with the coming of the three giantesses that the universe itself takes action to assist the gods in their mission with regards to the lives of men and brings forth three maidens to re-establish the balance of it all. This may appear off subject but let's consider the very powerful forces at work here. First of all the appearance of three beings, with less than good intentions, into a realm who has just won a great victory of independence and created a golden age is a foreboding of things to come. Things begin to be out of balance. How could it not be so with the sons of men if the palaces of the gods had become tainted? Much has happened in those 20 stanzas, much we have yet to decipher; then, we come back to two, named, and very corrupting influences of men, magic and the love of gold. Gollveig and Heith and we are going to treat them as two different individuals because that is how they are presented. Not only in the Bellows translation but in the Thorpe Translation as we see here;

> 7. *The Æsir met*
> *on Ida's plain;*
> *they altar-steads and temples*

high constructed;

their strength they proved,

all things tried,

furnaces established,

precious things forged,

formed tongs,

and fabricated tools;

8. At tables played at home;

joyous they were;

to them was naught

the want of gold,

until there came

Thurs-maidens three,

all powerful,

from Jötunheim.

Again we have a golden age of youth and there enters into the realm three beings from Jotunheim. Here they are referred to as all powerful. And again we see an outline of the character of these two female deities;

25. She that war remembers,
the first on earth,
when Gullveig they
with lances pierced,
and in the high one´s hall
her burnt,
thrice burnt,
thrice brough her forth,
oft not seldom;

yet she still lives.

26. *Heidi they called her,*
whithersoe´r she came,
the well-forseeing Vala:
wolves she tamed,
magic arts she knew,
magic arts practiced;
ever was she the joy
of evil people.

These two beings, in both the Bellows and the Thorpe translation are hard to deal with for even the mighty gods. One, Gollveig, (the love of gold) is burned three times and three times returns and the other Heidi or Heith (the shining one) is a joy to evil people. How is this supposed to represent the beneficial and loving nature of our goddess Freya? It is not. All too often people will point out that this god or that goddess is just another aspect of Odin or Freya, call it a kenning and ignore the fantastic possibility of growth. It's easier that way and it's also a scapegoat for just about anyone who cannot fathom the depths of either his being or the lore. These are two of the three all powerful beings who hailed from Jotunheim. Who the third could be is anyone's guess and perhaps someday it will be revealed, I'll bet half of you have taken a guess and will start looking for justification shortly. I hope you find something that will allow you to write a bestseller. Heith's power is magic, whereby people may gain control of or control over ideas and objects minus the wisdom necessary to use it properly, they use it for selfish and self centered gains. This is not what the All Father had in mind when we were given good sense. And Gollveig represents greed and the gods know this.

This is not the healthy appreciation of prosperity and abundance which Freya represents, but the all consuming and overpowering love of gold. We have all read in the history books about the destruction of entire cultures to obtain more of it. Treasure hunters still seek it, miners have died to obtain it and the possession of it is merely another way to shoot straight to the top without having done the personal work to get there. How ironic that people will work themselves to death for a shortcut to wealth. They have worked hard, yes they have, but they have not grown.

Let's say you had an idea you held to be very valuable, it provides you with the promise of being independent and having authority over others. Perhaps you were the very first kid in school that had a car. Now imagine someone slashed the tires because someone said you were hot rodding around town with somebody else's girlfriend. What would you do? Most likely there would be a fight. Keep that in mind as we look at this situation mentioned in the Bellows translation;

23. on the host his spear | did Othin hurl,
Then in the world | did war first come;
the wall that girdled | the gods was broken,
and the field by the warlike | Wanes was trodden.

24. Then sought the gods | their assembly-
seats,
the holy ones, | and council held,
Whether the gods | should tribute give,
Or to all alike | should worship belong.

It is readily apparent that the Vanir
or the Wanes, as they are called here,
took care of business. But it does not say
that they did so because of the burning of
Gollveig, what it says is should the gods
give tribute or to all alike should worship

belong. The Thorpe translation offers a little bit of clarification but also suggests it is the Aesir who have been slighted, not the Vanir. And yet another good case can be made that it was neither of them that introduced a corrupting idea to the minds of men, but instead three giantesses that reveled in the discord they had sought. So let's make that case.

27. *Then went the powers all*
to their judgement-seats,
the all-holy gods,
and thereon held council,
whether the Æsir should
avenge the crime,

or all the gods

receive atonement.

28. Broken was the outer wall
of the Æsir´s burgh.
The Vanir, forseeing conflict
tramp oér the plains.
Odin cast (his spear),
and mid the people hurled it:
that was the first
warfare in the world.

The Vanir represent a great many things but they also represent the wealth of the Earth itself. Njord is a God of the Sea and all the treasures it may hold. Frey is also a god of abundance and prosperity, Freya herself is a goddess of love, prosperity, fertility and abundance, but as a safeguard against the "love of gold" she also carries the Brisingamen Gem, the very fires of human intellect. These three were the hostages exchanged to the Aesir after the great Aesir /Vanir war. The Vanir perhaps witnessed what they perceived as the threatening of their way of life, such was the corrupting influence of the love of gold. And they went to war over it. The more reasonable interpretation of it is that the Vanir had decided that the close ties with the earth and all that it produces were much more worthy of worship than the high minded ideals of the gods in their golden palaces. Or, remember that kid with the hot rod, actually he was driving a minivan with his sister and the rumors got all mixed up. The Aesir were taking action to protect that which they had worked so hard for. The actions of the Aesir to protect men from the love of gold and the ability to control the flows of energy by mankind were most likely very misunderstood by the Vanir. These ideas and the inherent power associated with them were the playing field of the Vanir. To watch another group attempt to destroy a version of these concepts must have appeared as quite an insult. The passion of Vanir overwhelmed the reason of the Aesir. Much like it does in each of us at times.

When it came time to exchange hostages the Aesir offered wisdom so that the Vanir might understand and the Vanir submitted prosperity and abundance so that all might have access to the wealth of the earth and the heavens in a reasonable fashion. But even after a lesson hard learned by both sides, the Vanir again reverted to being ruled by passion and rejected wisdom and higher learning and they have largely been lost from history. It is only the incorporation of a well rounded pantheon of gods which has enabled the All Father to create something which affirms and strengthens the gifts he and his brothers bestowed upon Ask and Embla so that they may grow and develop. This wisdom has allowed our lore and the ideas they contain to withstand the test of time and even thousands of years of non use.

It is with good reason the Aesir sought to destroy these female jotuns and the concepts they represent. There was great wisdom in doing so and the idea behind the entire story is one we will see repeated. It is a story of the trials and tribulations of growth. The entire epoch of the various lays, with a very biased proclamation, deals with the struggles one must overcome to achieve that which the gods desired to create when we were given spirit, sense, blood and goodly color. It is the groundwork which the Aesir use to help us understand the struggle of birth and the subsequent endeavor to achieve the respect of an adult. In this wisdom there is for us a foundation which accords an understanding of every aspect of personal growth right alongside the growth of the world and the universe itself.

Profit thou hast if thou hearest,
Great thy gain if thou learnest

The Havamal

Understand ye yet, or what?

The Voluspa

Questions and Answers

Wise shall he seem who well can question,
And also answer well;
Nought is concealed that men may say
Among the sons of men.

This stanza of the Havamal was not written with the idea of "Asatru is the religion with homework" in mind. Lots of people use it in this manner, but more often than not, the conversations at our get together celebrations become something like a spelling bee, a contest of sorts as to who may happen to know the most about our ancestral heritage. Most of the time this is done in an effort to justify their position or in an attempt to demonstrate their knowledge insofar as Asatru is concerned and perhaps as a way to seek the validation we all sometimes need. This is understandable as the question and answer scenario arises in the Gripisspo, the Alvismol, the Hyndluljoth, the Grimnismol, and the Vafthruthnismol, and the entirety of the Prose Edda is dedicated to this idea. The value of this knowledge cannot be understated. And to many Asatruars it is worn as a badge of honor, the effort they have put into learning about our ancestral ways and history. Knowledge should always be highly valued. A proving grounds of a sorts typical of the interchange between people who may have just met and come from opposite sides of the country or the world. Often times their personal study of the history and archeology of the tribes of Northern Europe will put professors to shame. Similarly, there have been countless millions of dollars spent to determine the authenticity of the history of the bible while, with a great deal of satisfaction, the amateur historian and professional alike already know a great deal about the cultures which produced the lore we now hold so dear.

Yet how is it that we know as much as we do about our culture and a great deal of theirs is in doubt and the big three religions of the world control nearly 4 billion people while we are celebrating the assembly of 200 people. The cost is one minor issue. Church is free, you can donate what you wish and there are a lot of people who will not blink an eye at making that $1000.00 seed of faith donation. Most of the Asatru events cost money, the registration, the travel, so on and so forth and even at that some folk will not even drive across town to raise a horn with others. Sometimes they may not like them; but all too often it's because they just don't want to. So one must ask; why is the question and answer situation so important to the traditions of the tribes of northern Europe? Why have we pursued it as we have and had no real luck in reclaiming the thing we know in our hearts is real and viable as a way of life? Well; we do need to bear in mind that for many generations it was an oral tradition. The same questions and answers are posed to different individuals using different gods and heroes over and over so they could be remembered. Ever wonder why? Just like most spiritual traditions, there is a message in there. But this knowledge has by and large been collected by adherents to this reborn ideology of Asatru as a way to appear important, not in an effort to uncover the greater spiritual truths in the question and answer sessions of the lore. The penetrating gaze of self examination has stopped at the point we may feel maximum gain with regards to whether or not our ego gets hurt and fallen very short of the mark insofar as an understanding of deeper spiritual meaning is concerned. Why would anyone wish to attend an event where a self styled leader spends a great deal of time patting him on the back because he understands the ceremony but not the reason behind it? How many times have you stood in a blot and waited for something special to happen? Looking for anything that would validate your standing in a circle with whatever group of people you find yourself in. To put it mildly there are a great many people who are not having the needs of their spiritual being met.

What is it about the same questions which are repeated in no less than 5 books of the Poetic Edda and the entire Prose Edda? Let's peruse a few of these and see if there is a pattern, a standard of development for the individual to be a part of the community in the now as well as when we ourselves become ancestors. We will start with a concept repeated often enough and yet is simple enough to comprehend.

    23. "Mundilferi is he   who begat the moon,
and fathered the flaming sun;
The round of heaven   each day they run,
To tell the time for men."

Vafthruthnismol

6. Then sought the gods their assembly-seats,
The holy ones, and council held;
Names then gave they   to noon and twilight,
Morning they named, and the waning moon,

Night and evening,   the years to number.

Voluspa

Thor spake:

14. "Answer me, Alvis!   Thou knowest all,

Dwarf, of the doom of men:

What call them the moon,   which men behold,

in each and every world?"

Alvis spake:

15. "'Moon' with men, 'Flame' the gods among,

'The Wheel' in the house of hell;

'The Goer' the giants, 'The Gleamer' the

dwarfs ,The elves 'The Teller of Time."

.   **Alvismol**

These three stanzas are an example of the understanding a person should possess of the telling of time and the seasons. Common knowledge a person should have for the type of scheduling necessary to observe the holy rites of Asatru and the seasons of planting, harvesting and hunting. Important enough to be told in these three different tales that are who knows how old and from where they originated. Something likes a common thread across the continent and history resembling our farmer's almanac of today. There is no challenge in accepting this idea to be very close to the truth. There is likewise no sacrifice necessary to accept it in your life and practice of faith. And yet each person in the community needs to know these things so that everyone is working on the same page. Real simple, right? In our ancient past, yes, it was. But today there are a few that want to argue even this primitive concept while extolling their understanding of a more complicated idea such as sumbel.

We have to ask ourselves if in understanding this little portion of the lore are we closer to meeting the needs of our spirit. Well it's a start, the barest fraction of one, for in that little set of passages we see the beginning of how old these oral traditions might really be. It is the old tale of how the sun and moon came to be and why they are up there. Well, to imagine an ancient people contemplating the two largest things in the sky being of service to others puts a whole new light on the concepts of hospitality and generosity that Tacitus speaks of. Keeping the idea of just how old these oral traditions may be allows us to develop a framework of how this knowledge helped a people build a civilization. People in civilizations, great or small, must to a degree demonstrate an economy of effort; they must know how and when to work together for the common good. Even in this simple tale the common ground of knowing that these celestial bodies were placed there to help them measure time gave them a measure of reassurance and hope that their hard work would not be in vain. That perhaps they would be able to affect some control over the long term outcome of a great many things. Isn't that what a great deal of this is all about; the hope that our deeds may be worthy enough to merit a blessing of some kind from the gods and our ancestors. Now you may think this seems simplistic or that too much is being read into an old adage; but you must also consider that it was very simple ideas of faith like this one which allowed our ancestors and ancient cultures the world over to build monuments we cannot build today.

Sometimes we find contained in the lore answers without questions, we are offered knowledge the adept student is quick to understand. In the Grimnismol and as well in the Prose Edda we find a description of the halls of Asgard. The names are powerful reminders of the strengths of our Gods. The focal point for an origination of the concepts we believe our gods to represent. Thor lives in Thruthheim, the place of might. Ullr lives in Ydalir or the Yew-Dales, the wood out of which bows were made. Freyr resides in Alfheim home of the fair, light elves. Valaskjolf, the Shelf of the Slain is Odins home, where

Hlithskjolf is located. He built this one himself. It is interesting to note that there is an entirely separate location mentioned in Glatsheim, the Place of Joy, where Valhalla is located and the fallen heroes go when he calls them. Saga has her home in Sokkvabekk, the sinking stream, which Odin visits each day to share tales or perhaps to tell tales over drinks from cups of gold. Who wouldn't want to be the object of such a discussion? Thrymheim, the home of clamor is now the home of Skathi, where her father used to reside and such a clamor she did indeed raise when her father's life was taken. Baldurs residence is Breithablik which is translated as wide shining and is free of anything impure. Pure, brilliant and free from evil, a hint of the hope we will soon be discussing in this book. Heimdall lives in Himinbjorg, Heavens Cliffs, a second place where we can be sure he can keep an eye on everything. Here is where it can be tricky, Freya has Folkvang as her own, the field of the folk which is sometimes referred to as being in her hall Sessrymnir meaning rich in seats.

Folkvang is where she takes the first half of the dead. I wrote a great deal about why this may be the case in my book *Love and Hate in Asatru*. There are scholars who would suggest it is because of a confusion between Frigga and Freya but this is most likely not the case. In a hall pillared with gold sits Forsetti who settles strife in such a manner that no one is upset with the ruling. Glitner is its name which means the shining, a ray of hope from Baldurs son. Noatun the "ships-haven" is Njorth's' home. Vithar also is mentioned as having a home in

Vithi known as a forest with high standing grass, a verdant location full of life.

The Prose Edda is somewhat more descriptive but it is almost as if they are telling us how the jewels are set in the crown of heaven known as Asgard. From those descriptions we can determine in our hearts and our minds eye a course, much like a mariner charts the nighttime sky, to guide the actions of our lives. Similarly the steeds or the manner in which these blessings or favors or exchange of gifts is to be delivered also have names and meanings. Sleipnir, the Slipper; Gladr, the bright of glad; Gyllir the golden; Glenr the starer; Skeidbrimir, the fleet courser; Silfrintoppr, Silver-top; Sinir, sinewy; Gisl, beam or ray; Falhofnir, the hairy hoof; Gulltoppr, gold top; Lettfeti the light stepper was burned with Baldur in his funeral pyre. Thor walks. Whenever we focus upon a deity and the benefits they each individually bring into our lives it may also be wise to remember exactly how you wish for these blessings to be introduced into your life. My point in putting this long list together is that even in the reading of it, many of you will have remembered and further solidified the ideas which represent the substance of our faith. Even if you consider them fanciful retellings from a later period the image was still produced. With each retelling and description of the sites, names and stories of Asgardians and men it also gave the Gothi a starting point where he may begin a tale or give instruction or better yet, offer wisdom which offered guidance to a people so that they may try and live a worthy life.

Many folk will say "But the Eddas are not a bible. You are taking this all to seriously and we would be better off with historic and archeological teachings" This comment in and of itself betrays the speakers misconception of faith and hints at that persons limited ability to meet standards in their life of their own volition. Not because they need be concerned with heaven and hell but because it is the right thing to do. Far too many scholars have thrown their hat into the ring so to speak with their knowledge of these old tales, and yet none of it has helped us move our faith to the forefront. Much of it has done just the opposite. It has allowed many people to proclaim a following of this faith before they even understand it. Usually they feel grateful that there is no longer any kind of accountability. Lots of them, and we all know a few, use it as an excuse to continue engaging in practices that are well outside the societal norms. There is confusion between the meaning of guilt and shame. And in that that fleeting moment of perceived freedom and the colorful descriptions of the acts and homes of the gods there is something akin to a spiritual experience for the spiritually bankrupt. For the moment they are free of guilt. Just when this new feeling begins to wear off, they see where long time heathen scholars promote understanding the history and ancestor worship over an Asatruars concept of the faith of our ancestors. It causes no end of a problem for all of those people who feel deep inside their hearts that this is a powerful and positive way of life. One that is worth living and for many it once again puts the promise of a good life back upon the horizon. Our focus should be upon the Eddas. It is the written expression of our oral tradition and it serves to root the fleeting feelings of spiritual and emotional fancy in to a solid place where the acorn may grow to be a mighty oak.

Runes

I ween that I hung | on the windy tree,

Hung there for nights full nine;

With the spear I was wounded, | and offered I

was

To Othin, myself to myself,

On the tree that none | may ever know

What root beneath it runs.

~ 60 ~

The Runes are a powerful thing. They originate from somewhere outside of or in between the known realms. There is the chance that they originate from the same location as the Norns themselves. In as much as the cosmos suffered from the introduction of the three giantesses and all the chaos they created, we find the Norns introduced to provide balance. Likewise as Odin himself suffered and hung upon the tree, without food and water, wounded from his own spear; a powerful symbol of masculinity. He too, found balance at the base of tree;

> 140. *None made me happy | with loaf or horn,*
> *And there below I looked;*
> *I took up the runes, | shrieking I took them,*
> *And forthwith back I fell.*

The how and why of the manner in which Odin claimed the runes for himself are a powerful reminder for us that we will also find a great deal of wisdom in surviving and enduring our own suffering. And we are also reminded of Odins success as well;

142. Then began I to thrive, | and wisdom to get,
I grew and well I was;
Each word led me on | to another word,
each deed to another deed.

And yet the most common misconception about the runes, which for all intents and purposes are the very keys to the universe itself, is that they are some kind of magic or good luck charm. If the Havamal was the only place they were mentioned as well as the efforts necessary to earn them, I could see how this might be the case. But this attitude continues in spite of the fact that they are mentioned, like many other important ideas, more than once in our lore.

The Rigsthula is a book people often misinterpret or even worse read it so as to fit an argument they wish to win or a point of some kind to prove. Some people say it is the different races, or that it is the different classes of people; both could be easily surmised from a cursory reading. But this is simply not the case. Rig (Heimdall) visits his first couple who are named Ai and Edda, which translates to Great Grandfather and Great Grandmother. This is what transpires;

4. A loaf of bread | did Edda bring,

Heavy and thick | and swollen with husks;

Forth on the table | she set the fare,

And broth for the meal | in a bowl there was.

(Calf's flesh boiled | was the best of the

dainties.)

5. Rig knew well | wise words to speak,

Thence did he rise, | made ready to sleep;

Soon in the bed | himself did he lay,

And on either side | the others were.

All too often the only thing we see in our minds eye is three people in one bed. But this is very much out of character according to Tacitus' description of the reverence the North men held the institution of marriage. So we must consider the esoteric meanings as well as the physical ones. If we are unable to do so we place ourselves on the same infirm footing as the deceitful one finds himself when he confronts the assembled Aesir. It is not a huge leap of reasoning to perceive the welcoming of the divine into our homes and lives and especially with regards to the blessing of our future generations. But this group was indeed a homely lot, with names such as "the-coarse", "the bird-legged", "the fat" and "the sluggard" it seems apparent they could use a little more help. And so it was given, this time to Affi and Amma, grandfather and grandmother. A generation removed from the first visit. It is highly likely given the names of the couples that this was a series of events that may have happened over a very long time. Likewise this couple was somewhat more advanced in their skills and intelligence and the manner in which they applied their faith to their lives. These are not the hoary host we find in the first meeting of the divine and humanity

15. There sat the twain, | and worked at their tasks:

The man hewed wood | for the weaver's beam;

His beard was trimmed, | o'er his brow a curl,

His clothes fitted close; | in the corner a chest.

16. The woman sat | and the distaff wielded,

At the weaving with arms | outstretched she worked;

On her head was a band, | on her breast a smock;

On her shoulders a kerchief | with clasps there was

These folk had children known as "freeman", "the strong" and "holder of land". The initial seed of faith had begun to flower and the second blessing of the divine produced people and ideas we are familiar with and hold valuable today. The daughters had names as lovely as the sons were strong.

But it is the third and last set of folk Fathir and Mothir who begin to truly resemble modern concepts of family and all the opportunity a strong family unit can provide.

30. Then Mothir brought | a broidered cloth,
Of linen bright, | and the board she covered;
And then she took | the loaves so thin,

And laid them, white | from the wheat, on the cloth.

31. Then forth she brought | the vessels full,
With silver covered, | and set before them,
Meat all browned, | and well-cooked birds;
In the pitcher was wine, | of plate were the cups,
So drank they and talked | till the day was gone

Hospitality and generosity of a home which makes us smile and think of our own. When the divine is reinforced into this marriage we finally find a person, like us, who can learn from his mistakes, endure suffering to earn wisdom and who is finally ready to learn the secrets of the runes. It took nine long nights of the divine dealing with humanity to produce a being of this caliber;

35. *To grow in the house | did Jarl begin,*
Shields he brandished, | and bow-strings wound,
Bows he shot, | and shafts he fashioned,
Arrows he loosened, | and lances wielded,
Horses he rode, | and hounds unleashed,
Swords he handled, | and sounds he swam.

36. *Straight from the grove | came striding Rig,*
Rig came striding, | and runes he taught him;
By his name he called him, | as son he claimed him,

Jarl learned the runes from Rig but it is his son who demonstrates to us that we too have what it takes to use the runes as the Gods intended.

43. *Soon grew up | the sons of Jarl,*
Beasts they tamed, | and bucklers rounded,
Shafts they fashioned, | and spears they shook.

44. *But Kon the Young | learned runes to use,*
Runes everlasting, | the runes of life;
Soon could he well | the warriors shield,
Dull the sword blade, | and still the seas.

45. *Bird-chatter learned he, | flames could he lessen.,*

Minds could quiet, | and sorrows calm;
The might and strength | of twice four men.

46. With Rig-Jarl soon | the runes he shared,
More crafty he was, | and greater his wisdom;
The right he sought, | and soon he won it,
Rig to be called, | and runes to know.

In all of those long generations of
men and their acceptance of the divine it
is not until now, with the men who knew
and shared with their sons the power of
the runes, the capability to ascend to a
higher spiritual plane or level of
existence. Almost on par with a god.
The runes allow that spark of the divine

within us to blaze into existence. This gives us a powerful reference to the might of the runes, a might we can use if we are skilled. It speaks to us of ever increasing stages of development in our own lives and hopefully puts the serious reverence one should have for these holy symbols.

But this is not all. There is one other reference to the ancient symbols which govern the flows of energy through the universe. That is the story of Sigurth and Brunhilde. Sigurth, we are told, begins his journey by acquiring skills and training unimpeded by the protectiveness of the parents. He is given assistance from Odin and soon begins his first great quest. His killing of the dragon Fafnir, the slaying of the great wyrm of ego with its voracious love of gold, allows Sigurth to identify treachery and deal with it. Once he has worked and gained victory over himself and the demons around him he ascends a hill with fires that appear to reach the heavens. Once he crosses that fire and finds his equal and partner, then he too begins to thrive and wisdom get.

5. "Beer I bring thee, | tree of battle,
Mingled of strength | and mighty fame;
Charms it holds | and healing signs,
Spells full good, | and gladness-runes."

* * * * * *

6. Winning-runes learn, | if thou longest to
win,
And the runes on thy sword-hilt write;
Some on the furrow, | and some on the flat,
And twice shalt thou call on Tyr.

7. Ale-runes learn, | that with lies the wife
Of another betray not thy trust;

On the horn thou shalt write, | and the backs of
thy hands,
And Need shalt mark on thy nails.
Thou shalt bless the draught, | and danger
escape,
And cast a leek in the cup;
(For so I know | thou never shalt see
Thy mead with evil mixed.)

8. Birth-runes learn, | if help thou wilt lend,
The babe from the mother to bring;
On thy palms shalt write them, | and round thy
joints,
And ask the fates to aid.

9. Wave-runes learn, | if well thou wouldst
shelter
The sail-steeds out on the sea;
On the stem shalt thou write, | and the steering
blade,
And burn them into the oars;
Though high be the breakers, | and black the
waves,
Thou shalt safe the harbor seek.

10. Branch-runes learn, | if a healer wouldst be,
And cure for wounds wouldst work;

On the bark shalt thou write, | and on trees
that be
With boughs to the eastward bent.

11. Speech-runes learn, | that none may seek
To answer harm with hate;

Well he winds | and weaves them all,
And sets them side by side,
At the judgment-place, | when justice there
The folk shall fairly win.

12. Thought-runes learn, | if all shall think
Thou art keenest minded of men.

13. Them Hropt arranged, | and them he wrote,
And them in thought he made,

Out of the draught | that down had dropped
From the head of Heithdraupnir,
And the horn of Hoddrofnir.

14. On the mountain he stood | with Brimir's
sword,
On his head the helm he bore;
Then first the head | of Mim spoke forth,
And words of truth it told.

15. He bade write on the shield | before the
shining goddess,
On Arvak's ear, | and on Alsvith's hoof,
On the wheel of the car | of Hrungnir's killer,

On Sleipnir's teeth, | and the straps of the
sledge.

16. On the paws of the bear, | and on Bragi's
tongue,

On the wolf's claws bared, | and the eagle's
beak,
On bloody wings, | and bridge's end,
On freeing hands | and helping foot-prints.

17. On glass and on gold, | and on goodly
charms,
In wine and in beer, | and on well-loved seats,
On Gungnir's point, | and on Grani's breast,
On the nails of Norns, | and the night-owl's
beak.

* * * * * *

18. Shaved off were the runes | that of old were
written,
And mixed with the holy mead,
And sent on ways so wide;
So the gods had them, | so the elves got them,

And some for the Wanes so wise,
And some for mortal men.

19. Beech-runes are there, | birth-runes are
there,
And all the runes of ale,

And the magic runes of might;
Who knows them rightly | and reads them true,
Has them himself to help;
Ever they aid,
Till the gods are gone.

We once again see the mingling of
the divine between two people who do
not compromise the quality of their
being; they share their wisdom and love
and accept the divine to be a part of it. I
have always loved this tale and the
knowledge that it affords us. The beauty

of love and the seemingly limitless accomplishments a couple of people who love each other can achieve. Notice that the courage and boldness comes from the male, much like Odin, but that the understanding of the ways of the universe originates with feminine, similar to Frigga. There is a lot to think about in all of it. These runes offer us an avenue, or maybe you could even consider them signposts along the route the Norns have allocated us to travel in life. Odin suffered to get them, knowing that if he was lost the cosmos would balance itself out and it did, when all seemed to be failing and in the truest fashion of Odin he earned the runes for us all. It has been shown that they are a benefit to the gods, to the individual and to the couple as well. The beauty of this romantic tale between Sigurth and Brunhilde is not lost upon us and we see the terrible curse and the destruction that the love of gold has wrought upon men and why Odin sought to destroy it in Asgard long, long ago. These struggles and the Wyrd woven throughout the Eddas are here to reinforce upon us that we are not alone and that the Gods are on our side.

The Ascension of Odin

As we can see from the incredible actions of the gods in dealing with the poisonous influence of three Jotunar, there are great lengths to which Odin will go to obtain wisdom. He will test what he already knows and seek even more. These are most often perceived as selfish actions. But there is another frequently recurring theme in the Eddas which bears a great deal of discussion. That is the making of a god as well as the failure of one to make the grade.

But let's first discuss the rest of the story with regards to Odin and his constant quest for wisdom.

But under that root which turns toward the Rime-Giants is Mimirs Well, wherein wisdom and understanding are stored; and he is called Mimirs, who keeps the well. He is full of ancient lore, since he drinks of the well from the Gjallar-Horn. Thither came Allfather and craved one drink of the well; but he got it not until he had laid his eye in pledge. So says Völuspá:

All know I, Odin, | where the eye thou hiddest,
In the wide-renowned | well of Mímir;
Mímir drinks mead | every morning
From Valfather's wage. | Wit ye yet, or what?

It should not go unnoticed that the Gjallar-horn is usually ascribed to belonging to Heimdall. Also worthy of mention is that Mímir is quite likely his maternal uncle.

141. Nine mighty songs | I got from the son
Of Bolthorn, Bestla's father;
And a drink I got | of the goodly mead
Poured out from Othrörir.

Also worth remembering is the fact that this particular well of wisdom is under the root which runs towards the land of the rime giants. Remember that the rivers which flow thru that land are frozen. The wisdom and life of the flow of water is locked up. And yet the value of this water is such that it requires the sacrifice of an eye to obtain just one drink of it. Many times I have found wisdom near a road that leads to nowhere and each time it has cost me, sometimes dearly. But Odin does not let this deter him from seeking wisdom in all the places he is able to. Of course Odin exchanges him after the Aesir/Vanir war and we all know the outcome. The wisdom of Mímir is perceived as a crutch to Hoenir and his head cut off, the Vanir felt that they had been cheated in the exchange. Odin then preserves this head and uses it even unto the day of Ragnarok. Mímir was sent as an exchange for Kvasir the wisest man in Vanaheim. His tale is also of interest.

they appointed a peace-meeting between them and established peace in this way: they each went to a vat and spat their spittle therein. Then at parting the gods took that peace-token and would not let it perish, but shaped thereof a man. This man is called Kvasir, and he was so wise that none could question him concerning anything but that he knew the solution. He went up and down the earth to give instruction to men;

Kvasir was killed by dwarves who were in turn set upon by the giant Suttung. This is an opportunity for Odin and he takes it.

 Bölverkr proceeded to the place where Gunnlöd was, and lay with her three nights; and then she gave him leave to drink three draughts of the mead. In the first draught he drank every drop out of Ódrerir; and in the second, he emptied Bodn; and in the third, Són; and then he had all the mead. Then he turned himself into the shape of an eagle and flew as furiously as he could; but when Suttungr saw the eagle's flight, he too assumed the fashion of an eagle and flew after him. When the Æsir saw Odin flying, straightway they set out their vats in the court; and when Odin came into Ásgard, he spat up *the mead into the vats. Nevertheless he came so near to being caught by Suttungr that he sent some mead backwards, and no heed was taken of this: whosoever would might have that, and we call that the poetaster's part. But Odin gave the mead of Suttungr to the Æsir and to those men who possess the ability to compose.*

So now, Odin seems to have all the keys. And he has sacrificed a great deal to earn it. He has also picked up the art of Seidhr from Freya and remember that Frigga knows all things as such that Odin knows. Did he tell her or was she already in possession of such knowledge? This is a powerful indicator of the strength of the divine feminine. The fact that Odin has managed to weave a web of Wyrd which would allow him to obtain the various sources of wisdom throughout the realms and comprehending these actions, is the key to unlocking a more thorough understanding of ourselves and the universe.

In the midst of all of this; we are also made aware that he is also choosing which gods to make and surround himself with. He is already aware that he will not survive the Ragnarok. He has been to places and done things that are not worthy to be carried forward. His actions are a sacrifice of self on a level few of us will be able to mentally digest in our current form. But emotionally we are all able to see that he is preparing the way for his sons and grandsons and daughters to move well past where he is in their own golden age.

Now matter where you place Tyr in the pantheon of the Aesir, we do have a tale which seems to illustrate a being that did not start out at the top. In the Hymiskvitha these two stanzas deserve a second look.

*8. The youth found his grandam, | that
greatly he loathed,
And full nine hundred | heads she had;
But the other fair | with gold came forth,
And the bright-browed one | brought beer to
her son.*

*9. "Kinsman of giants, | beneath the kettle
Will I set ye both, | ye heroes bold;
For many a time | my dear-loved mate
To guests is wrathful | and grim of mind."*

For some people it is easier to assume
that the mother, the one who is fair with
gold and bright browed may be from a
race of gods whether it is the Aesir or
Vanir we cannot be certain. Or she may
well have been just like Gerdhr, a
diamond in the rough. I think the latter
is more likely and makes more sense with

respect to the parables often contained in these tales. What it means is that at some point in his existence Tyr stepped up and out of the mold and away from the simple beings that bore him. He became more than his parents and he did so in such a way that he could be counted an equal among the gods. We have seen how the runes enabled at least one being to do this very thing. The how and why of Tyrs' arrival have been lost for a very long time. But there are others.

Hercules is one example, at least in the popular versions of his tales. But I think we can all agree that having Tyr at your side for the final battle is one of those things which go in the plus column. But there are others, some are a plus all on their own, such as Skadi, and some are a representation of the sons they may bear, such as Rindr and some are about what you value and what you will make your sacrifices for. Love or War and we see in the case of Gerdhr and Freyr. I have written extensively about all of them in my book *Love and Hate in Asatru*, which also goes on to outline the one being, who though he had every opportunity, failed to make the grade and ended up being rejected. He failed to comprehend and take action on the deeper meanings of all the things going on around him. Be that as it may we have a couple of deities and their ascension to godhood and the remarkable parallels to becoming a man or woman which bear closer scrutiny. Keep in mind that the chess board is already set in play and Odin has gone to great lengths to learn the rules. With Skadhi, he picks a champion, with Rindr, he chooses a princess to bear a son, Vali, who grows to manhood within a day and takes revenge for the slaying of his half brother by killing a blind god. Think of the mental gymnastics in assuming the mantle of adulthood involved with that little task. But isn't it usually the young who are so prone to acts of violent passion? We see where Hermódr must traverse the dangerous corridors between the realms and the father gives to the son a fine symbol of masculinity with which to handle the task. Notice these gods are undertaking tasks which mature and strengthen them for what is to come. But one cannot really blame Odin; his supposed blood brother did coerce and lie to another god to murder his son. I would be stacking the deck as well. His son is Thor constantly seeking out giants to slay and is ever the defender of Midgard. Look at what he is up against. While the fight may be unwinnable, the festering poison introduced into Asgard by the deceitful one and his offspring as well as three powerful giantesses must be put to a stop. Much like in our own lives. Once we have allowed even a toehold of destructive behavior to operate with regards to our dealings with family and friends, business and the public, it usually takes a dramatic effort to be rid of it.

Ragnarok

All of these threads of the ideas we find contained within the lore have a bearing upon how the universe operates and how we may grow. It is archetypal and is perhaps some of the finest writing of its kind with regards to human development. The fact that these stories sing to us in a fashion which our very souls seem to have an ear for is no accident. It is larger than life and captures our imagination and just when we are about to toss out the baby with the bathwater we see the hint of something written down long ago that will help us today. The concept and the story of Ragnarok is no different. It is hinted at in the Voluspa, which as we have seen, is the beginning of so many threads which run through the Eddas.

32. I saw for Baldr, | the bleeding god,
The son of Othin, | his destiny set:

Famous and fair | in the lofty fields,
Full grown in strength | the mistletoe stood.

33. From the branch which seemed | so slender and fair
Came a harmful shaft | that Hoth should hurl;
But the brother of Baldr | was born ere long,
And one night old | fought Othin's son.
34. His hands he washed not, | his hair he combed not,
Till he bore to the bale-blaze | Baldur's foe.
But in Fensalir | did Frigg weep sore

For Valhall's need: | would you know yet more?

Just take a look at how many beings are taking a role in this drama; they are all being affected by the wounded ego of the mishchievious one when he tries to kill what he cannot measure up to. We see this same type of situation, though not nearly as dramatic, play out with the polite character assassination we often over hear at work or on the television or the internet. A life is put on hold, a mother weeps, a son is rushed to manhood, and another son has to endure the trials of hell to try and assuage his mother and fathers grief on his own journey of discovery. We have all seen so many variations of this type of situation it's like a rubiks cube of human emotion. Yet here it is thousands of years old and we stand the chance to learn something of faith in these words which we can use in our own lives today. Paying attention to these and many other lessons contained within the lore has afforded me an avenue to pursue spiritual growth. When I see someone decry the Eddas as not being worthy of consideration or that they have no value at all; I have to wonder why someone would listen to anything they have to say much less how they can accurately call it Asatru. For I see, very plainly, the ideas, the examples and the demonstration of what it takes to grow spiritually and what happens when you do not. But I digress; we are speaking of the death of Baldur, the loss of innocence and the long time it takes to heal these types of wounds

The matter which has been spoken of in the Voluspa is of such concern that we have what is known as Baldrs Drauma.

1. Once were the gods | together met,
And the goddesses came | and council held,
And the far-famed ones | the truth would find,
Why baleful dreams | to Baldr had come.

Odin agrees with this all powerful council and sets out on his steed, Sleipnir, to enter into the gates of Hels domain to find an answer to protect his son. What father would not do the same if he had the chance? He seeks out a seeress who has long since passed and interestingly enough Vegtam (the wanderer) refers to her as the mother of giants three.

Othin spake:
8. "Wise-woman, cease not! | I seek from thee
All to know | that I fain would ask:
Who shall the bane | of Baldr become,
and steal the life | from Othin's son?"

The Wise-Woman spake:
9. "Hoth thither bears | the far-famed branch,
He shall the bane | of Baldr become,
And steal the life | from Othin's son.
Unwilling I spake, | and now would be still."

Othin spake:
10. "Wise-woman, cease not! | I seek from thee
All to know | that I fain would ask:
Who shall vengeance win | for the evil work,
Or bring to the flames | the slayer of Baldr?"

The Wise-Woman spake:
11. "Rind bears Vali | in Vestrsalir,
And one night old | fights Othin's son;

His hands he shall wash not, | his hair he shall
comb not,
Till the slayer of Baldr | he brings to the

~ 108 ~

flames.
Unwilling I spake, | and now would be still."

Othin spake:
12. "Wise-woman, cease not! | I seek from thee
All to know | that I fain would ask:
What maidens are they | who then shall weep,
And toss to the sky | the yards of the sails?"

The Wise-Woman spake:
13. "Vegtam thou art not, | as erstwhile I
thought;
Othin thou art, | the enchanter old."

Othin spake:
"No wise-woman art thou, | nor wisdom hast;
Of giants three | the mother art thou."

All of his efforts have been for

naught. This is stuff he already knows.

But it is a powerful example of the love a

father has for his son and what a son may be called upon to do to protect and safeguard his own progeny someday.

You see, like most of the Eddas, there is a story between the lines which works on just about every imaginable level of our existence.

There is an ebb and flow of these tales which resemble so much of our own lives. The death of Baldur is no different. It is something akin to the loss of innocence and has a great deal of bearing upon the ceremonies of man and woman making. Not only for Baldur and

Nanna, but also for Hermódr and Fulla and the changes necessary for Odin and Frigga to undergo are some that all parents feel to a degree from the time a child first heads off to school to the time they leave for college or for the service. And some few will be struck by the tragedy of a loss hopefully few of us will ever have to endure. Those folk will find guidance in the depths of these tales coupled with their own personal anguish and wisdom which may enable them to make it through one more day.

Baldur is the beautiful youth, just like all of us were at one time or another. Insults and injuries could be shaken off or had no effect upon us at all. Until the one fateful day when a realization or a doubt begins to take root. Usually this comes in the form of a wounded ego telling us we don't quite measure up in some fashion. The same thing can be said of the chief back biter of the gods, he also cannot measure up to the stunning brilliance of Baldur and he whispers in the ear of a outsider, a blind god, whose inability to see the truth of the situation steals the light out of our hearts and the heavens at the same time. Anyone who has ever gone through a divorce or suffered the heart rending loss of a child will be familiar with that little voice which whispers to our psyche, "you weren't good enough" the origination of this voice can never see the truth of the situation and wears us down. Sometimes it kills the light inside of us and the scars upon our heart cannot or will not heal.

And when that was done and made known, then it was a diversion of Baldur's and the Æsir, that he should stand up in the Thing, and all the others should some shoot at him, some hew at him, some beat him with stones; but whatsoever was done hurt him not at all, and that seemed to them all a very worshipful thing.

"But when Loki Laufeyarson saw this, it pleased him ill that Baldr took no hurt. He went to Fensalir to Frigg, and made himself into the likeness of a woman. Then Frigg asked if that woman knew what the Æsir did at the Thing. She said that all were shooting at Baldr, and moreover, that he took no hurt. Then said Frigg: 'Neither weapons nor trees may hurt Baldr: I have taken oaths of them all.' Then the woman asked: 'Have all things taken oaths to spare Baldr?' and Frigg answered: 'There grows a tree-sprout alone westward of Valhall: it is called Mistletoe; I thought it too young to ask the oath of.'

Then straightway the woman turned away; but Loki took Mistletoe and pulled it up and went to the Thing.

"Hödr stood outside the ring of men, because he was blind. Then spake Loki to him: 'Why dost thou not shoot at Baldr?' He answered: 'Because I see not where Baldr is; and for this also, that I am weaponless.' Then said Loki: 'Do thou also after the manner of other men, and show Baldr honor as the other men do. I will direct thee where he stands; shoot at him with this wand.' Hödr took Mistletoe and shot at Baldr, being guided by Loki: the shaft flew through Baldr, and he fell dead to the earth; and that was the greatest mischance that has ever befallen among gods and men.

At some point in our lives this same event happens to us. We lose our innocence, and the innocence of youth is a thing treasured the entire world over. Make no mistake, there is evil involved in the destruction of it. But it is what happens next in this tale which offers us true guidance.

But when the Æsir tried to speak, then it befell first that weeping broke out, so that none might speak to the others with words concerning his grief. But Odin bore that misfortune by so much the worst, as he had most perception of how great harm and loss for the Æsir were in the death of Baldr.

"Now when the gods had come to themselves, Frigg spake, and asked who there might be among the Æsir who would fain have for his own all her love and favor: let him ride the road to Hel, and seek if he may find Baldr, and offer Hel a ransom if she will let Baldr come home to Asgard. And he is named Hermódr the Bold, Odin's son, who undertook that embassy. Then Sleipnir was taken, Odin's steed, and led forward; and Hermódr mounted on that horse and galloped off.*

The Allfather is struck with grief beyond words', the great mother of the Aesir offers all of her love and favor to a champion. And Hermódr takes this opportunity to become a man as it were.

The love and strength of a mother, the great symbol of masculinity which is Sleipnir send him on his way and an arduous journey lay in front of him, which is to find and indentify the great promise of manhood.

"Now this is to be told concerning Hermódr, that he rode nine nights through dark dales and deep, so that he saw not before he was come to the river Gjöll and rode onto the Gjöll-Bridge; which bridge is thatched with glittering gold. Módgudr is the maiden called who guards the bridge; she asked him his name and race, saying that the day before there had ridden over the bridge five companies of dead men; 'but the bridge thunders no less under thee alone, and thou

hast not the color of dead men. Why ridest thou hither on Hel-way?' He answered: 'I am appointed to ride to Hel to seek out Baldr. Hast thou perchance seen Baldr on Hel-way?' She said that Baldr had ridden there over Gjöll's Bridge,-'but down and north lieth Hel-way.'

"Then Hermódr rode on till he came to Hel-gate; he dismounted from his steed and made his girths fast, mounted and pricked him with his spurs; and the steed leaped so hard over the gate that he came nowise near to it. Then Hermódr rode home to the hall and dismounted from his steed, went into the hall, and saw sitting there in the high-seat Baldr, his brother; and Hermódr tarried there overnight. At morn Hermódr prayed Hel that Baldr might ride home with him, and told her how great weeping was

~ 119 ~

among the Æsir. But Hel said that in this wise it should be put to the test, whether Baldr were so all-beloved as had been said: 'If all things in the world, quick and dead, weep for him, then he shall go back to the Æsir; but he shall remain with Hel if any gainsay it or will not weep.' Then Hermódr arose; but Baldr led him out of the hall, and took the ring Draupnir and sent it to Odin for a remembrance. And Nanna sent Frigg a linen smock, and yet more gifts, and to Fulla a golden finger-ring.

"Then Hermódr rode his way back, and came into Asgard, and told all those tidings which he had seen and heard.

He braves the wastelands of life, crosses the mighty river, comes face to face with a powerful feminine figure and keeps on going; he encounters the dead and the monsters of Hels realm. Almost like a walk through the poorest most crime ridden parts of town isn't it? Finally, after he has passed his tests he finds his brother doing the same thing he is. He is accepting the trials in front him which will make him a man. These brothers talk the night through and discuss what may be coming up in life. When it is time to go, Baldur sends the ring Draupnir a symbol of wealth, back to the rightful owner who is the king of

Asgard. He will earn his own way so to speak. Nanna sends to Frigga the linen smock which is the common garb for all young men of those times, made by their mothers as they headed off to fight in wars and suffer long journeys. This is a powerful token which represents the fact that Baldur has accepted a new feminine into his life and cut the apron strings so to speak. Baldur is no momma's boy. He and his wife send back gifts which signal that they have accepted the challenge to grow into fine adults no matter what course is set in front of them. They will literally pass through hel together and come out the stronger because of it. Hermódr sees this and accepts the responsibility, already coming as far as he has, to achieve adulthood/godhood as responsibly as his brother is trying to do. Fulla, the immature feminine, receives a sign of hope in the form of a finger ring; a ring to remember that she can do it too and it will be ok.

Hermódr' heroic return and the understanding he has received from his brother along with his gifts, signals to the world how and where to find the evil we should all avoid. Think of the changes of all of those people, they form a parallel which astounds the imagination when you realize that so much of human nature has remained the same since very ancient times.

So much of my own life has been this way. As a young man who was full of promise I dared and challenged the world. But before I even got a chance to strut my stuff, drugs disabled my ambition. I had to take the very long road down before I could find anything which would give me the hope to try it again. I've suffered bouts of drug addiction which ruined not only my, but everyone around me life as well. I've accomplished this three times in my life. It was not until I found Asatru and I could almost feel the parallels in my own life to these ancient tales that I found a new way to live. I found it in the Eddas. It wasn't difficult. I've poured over all of the volumes again and again, studied to become a Gothi and worked tirelessly after I come home from work to build not only the AFA but my organization Nanna's Hearth as well. Not in order that I may be proven right but that other people will have the chance to live as good a life as I enjoy now. Ragnarok is the introduction of something into our lives when we are young which wounds us, and instead of working our way through the dark times and truly incorporating the wisdom we are earning into our lives, we limp along much like the gods, wounded and suffering the pain of loss and allowing the knowledge of what's to come or what we've been thru to cast a shadow over everything we do. At some point in your life there will be something very difficult you will have to deal with. When it is all said and done will you return as a shining example of what the lore can teach you, or will your return be marked with righteous indignation in lieu of spiritual growth? These Eddas are thousands of years old. Trust in them as our ancestors did.

The Return of Hope

This is the part which makes heathens cringe. For very obvious reasons. The wound which Christianity has inflicted upon the human psyche is so damaging, so poisonous, that anything which resembles or even hints at a being who returns from the dead to become god causes within us a knee jerk reaction to reject it, outright, wholesale, it doesn't matter. But that's where the poison corrupts the wound. As I mentioned in my *Inguz; Developing the God Seed*, that very storyline has been repeated at least sixteen times, that I know of, all over the world. So there has got to be something more to it than just copying the Christians so they don't cut your head off when you are writing it all down.

While my analogies may be anecdotal, I am firmly convinced that I have not created any new emotion which has not been felt by the rest of humanity. That bond is what helps to give these tales the strength to last the ages, where they were created helps give them a flavor we can all digest. The poison I was talking about is like someone spilling the salt on your meal. But this is a faith so let's treat it as such and find the manner in which we may embrace and allow our unique faith to enfold us into its familiar light. Just a like a warm hug from a grandma. I've know some very tough men who were raised by their grandmas who would not under any circumstances allow you to say a thing negative about those fine matriarchs we have all loved at one time. Why on earth would you allow anyone to determine how you are going to perceive the tales of our grandmother Edda?

The one thing which truly saddens me is that we never really know what happens to the Asynjur. Ragnarok in itself is a very complicated story to try and digest, but the promises of what is to come on a universal as well as a personal level are just as difficult. As we have read in the last chapter it is a description of all of the events which occur to deal with a compromise of principle and ego in our youth and the youth of the cosmos. Those things always catch up to us. But it is also a reminder that if we fight as long and as hard as we can, if we

reinforce the very best aspect of
ourselves, despite the world burning
down around us, taking our love and our
pride and our egos with it, what rises
from the ashes; having been born of fire,
is tempered and strong, full of confidence
and the promise of a new day.

Brothers shall strive | and slaughter each other;
Own sisters' children | shall sin together;
Ill days among men, | many a whoredom:
An axe-age, a sword-age, | shields shall be cloven;
A wind-age, a wolf-age, | ere the world totters.

We are given a sign of the times.
Some of us who have lived through

harder times have seen this kind of dissension all around us. Most folks nowadays call it drama. This is not to say I think the world is ending but it most certainly is changing. After that the great story of the battle of Ragnarok is told.

Then shall happen what seem great tidings: the Wolf shall swallow the sun; and this shall seem to men a great harm. Then the other wolf shall seize the moon, and he also shall work great ruin; the stars shall vanish from the heavens. Then shall come to pass these tidings also: all the earth shall tremble so, and the crags, that trees shall be torn up from the earth, and the crags fall to ruin; and all fetters and bonds shall be broken and rent. Then shall Fenris-Wolf get loose; then the sea shall gush forth upon the land, because the Midgard Serpent stirs in giant wrath and advances up onto the land. Then that too shall happen, that Naglfar shall be loosened, the ship which is so named. (It is made of dead men's nails; wherefore a warning is desirable, that if a man die with unshorn nails, that man adds much material to the ship Naglfar, which gods and men were fain to have finished late.) Yet in this sea-flood Naglfar shall float. Hrymr is the name of the giant who steers Naglfar. Fenris-Wolf shall advance with gaping mouth, and his lower jaw shall be against the earth, but the upper against heaven,--he would gape yet more if there were room for it; fires blaze from his eyes and nostrils. The Midgard Serpent shall blow venom so that he shall sprinkle all the air and water; and he is very terrible, and shall be on one side of the Wolf. In this din shall the heaven be cloven, and the Sons of Múspell ride thence: Surtr shall ride first, and both before him and after him burning fire; his sword is exceeding good: from it radiance shines brighter than from the sun; when they ride over Bifröst, then the bridge shall break, as has been told before. The Sons of Múspell shall go forth to that field which is called Vígrídr, thither shall come Fenris-Wolf also and the Midgard Serpent; then Loki and Hrymr shall come there also, and with him all the Rime-Giants. All the champions of Hel follow Loki; and the Sons of Múspell shall have a company by themselves, and it shall be very bright. The field Vígrídr is a hundred leagues wide each way.

"When these tidings come to pass, then shall Heimdallr rise up and blow mightily in the Gjallar-Horn, and awaken all the gods; and they shall hold council together. Then Odin shall ride to Mímir's Well and take counsel of Mímir for himself and his host. Then the Ash of Yggdrasil shall tremble, and nothing then shall be without fear in heaven or in earth. Then shall the Æsir put on their war-weeds, and all the Champions, and advance to the field: Odin rides first with the gold helmet and a fair birnie, and his spear, which is called Gungnir. He shall go forth against Fenris-Wolf, and Thor stands forward on his other side, and can be of no avail to him, because he shall have his hands full to fight against the

Midgard Serpent. Freyr shall contend with Surtr and a hard encounter shall there be between them before Freyr falls: it is to be his death that he lacks that good sword of his, which he gave to Skírnir. Then shall the dog Garmr be loosed, which is bound before Gnipa's Cave: he is the greatest monster; he shall do battle with Týr and each become the other's slayer. Thor shall put to death the Midgard Serpent, and shall stride away nine paces from that spot; then shall he fall dead to the earth, because of the venom which the Snake has blown at him. The Wolf shall swallow Odin; that shall be his ending But straight thereafter shall Vídarr stride forth and set one foot upon the lower jaw of the Wolf: on that foot he has the shoe, materials for which have been gathering throughout all time. (They are the scraps of leather which men cut out: of their shoes at toe or heel; therefore he who desires in his heart to come to the Æsir's help should cast those scraps away.) With one hand he shall seize the Wolf's upper jaw and tear his gullet asunder; and that is the death of the Wolf. Loki shall have battle with

Heimdallr and each is the slayer of the other.
Then straightway shall Surtr cast fire over the
earth and burn all the world; so is said
in Völuspá:

> High blows Heimdallr, | the horn
> is aloft;
> Odin communes | with Mímir's
> head;
> Trembles Yggdrasill's | towering
> Ash;
> The old tree wails | when the
> Ettin is loosed.

> What of the Æsir? | What of the
> Elf-folk?
> All Jötunheim echoes, | the Æsir
> are at council;
> The dwarves are groaning |
> before their stone doors,
> Wise in rock-walls; | wit ye yet,
> or what?

> Hrymr sails from the east, | the
> sea floods onward;

The monstrous Beast | twists in
mighty wrath;
The Snake beats the waves, | the
Eagle is screaming;
The gold-neb tears corpses, |
Naglfar is loosed.

From the east sails the keel; |
come now Múspell's folk
Over the sea-waves, | and Loki
steereth;
There are the warlocks | all with
the Wolf,--
With them is the brother | of
Býleistr faring.

Surtr fares from southward |
with switch-eating flame;
On his sword shimmers | the sun
of the war-gods;
The rocks are falling, | and fiends
are reeling,
Heroes tread Hel-way, | heaven
is cloven.

Then to the Goddess | a second
grief cometh,
When Odin fares | to fight with
the Wolf,
And Beli's slayer, | the bright
god, with Surtr;
There must fall | Frigg's beloved.

Odin's son goeth | to strife with
the Wolf,--
Vídarr, speeding | to meet the
slaughter-beast;
The sword in his hand | to the
heart he thrusteth
Of the fiend's offspring; avenged
is his Father.

Now goeth Hlödyn's | glorious
son
Not in flight from the Serpent, |
of fear unheeding;
All the earth's offspring | must
empty the homesteads,
When furiously smiteth |
Midgard's defender.

The sun shall be darkened, | earth sinks in the sea,--
Glide from the heaven | the glittering stars;
Smoke-reek rages | and reddening fire:
The high heat licks | against heaven itself.

I had briefly considered leaving this lengthy tale out of the book. But in reading it and enjoying a certain amount of insight concerning what the Gods represent to me and to the universe, I always find myself engaging in the mental gymnastics of indentifying the concepts each God and monster represents. It seems as if the ancient wounds and the weapons which were forged for them by a sinister element cause their downfall. In compromising their principles they sowed the seeds of their own destruction. We are no different. A little lie here and there, a deceitful action or a cowardly act, even sometimes our inability to show compassion and our over reactions stemming from anger. A failure on our part to realize that that the actions of others do not mitigate the quality of the people we are. It is another aspect of Baldurs acceptance of his fate and Nanna with him. Notice it is Hodr who returns with Baldur. Their life journey through realms of Hel, absent the constant presence of the divine which all the others have enjoyed, has helped him to work harder to become what he and they are supposed to become. That idea, that even though we feel alone, we are still a part of something great is reinforced in the Hyndluljoth where we see Freya escorting one her faithful to meet with a creature who is considered to be much less than man or goddess. Almost as if to tell us that if even these simple beings can tell you that they know the ancestors on our your side, that you are part of something great and that someday you will return to it. It is a tale which also reinforces the idea that even though we may be physically separated from the divine, they are still very much on our side, in layman's terms we are being told we are worthy of everything we could aspire to be. Baldr, Nanna, Hodr and Ottar are examples of this. Take that belief to heart and aspire to greatness yourself. These old tales tell us we have what it takes especially if we have faith.

10. "For me a shrine | of stones he made,--
And now to glass | the rock has grown;--
Oft with the blood | of beasts was it red;
In the goddesses ever | did Ottar trust.

Now we come to the heart of the matter, the idea that after all we have been through, there is something good to come. The return or the survival of the best of the Gods.

> *"Shall any of the gods live then, or shall there be then any earth or heaven?" Hárr answered: "In that time the earth shall emerge out of the sea, and shall then be green and fair; then shall the fruits of it be brought forth unsown. Vídarr and Váli shall be living, inasmuch as neither sea nor the fire of Surtr shall have harmed them; and they shall dwell at Ida-Plain, where Ásgard was before. And then*

the sons of Thor, Módi and Magni, shall come there, and they shall have Mjöllnir there. After that Baldr shall come thither, and Hödr, from Hel; then all shall sit down together and hold speech. with one another, and call to mind their secret wisdom, and speak of those happenings which have been before: of the Midgard Serpent and of Fenris-Wolf. Then they shall find in the grass those golden chess-pieces which the Æsir had had; thus is it said:

> In the deities' shrines | shall dwell
> Vídarr and Váli,
>   When the Fire of Surtr is
> slackened;
> Módi and Magni | shall have
> Mjöllnir
>   At the ceasing of Thor's strife.

In the place called Hoddmímir's Holt there shall lie hidden during the Fire of Surtr two of mankind, who are called thus: Líf and Lífthrasir, and for food they shall have the morning-dews. From these folk shall come so numerous an offspring that all the world shall be peopled, even as is said here:

> Líf and Lífthrasir, | these shall lurk hidden
>> In the Holt of Hoddmímir;
> The morning dews | their meat shall be;
>> Thence are gendered the generations.

And it may seem wonderful to thee, that the sun shall have borne a daughter not less fair than herself; and the daughter shall then tread in the steps of her mother, as is said here:

> The Elfin-beam | shall bear a daughter,
>> Ere Fenris drags her forth;
> That maid shall go, | when the great gods die,
>> To ride her mother's road.

Vidar and Vali, Módi and Magni along with Mjolnir, Baldr and Hodr are released by Hel and also a daughter of Sunna is spoken of to return after the fire consumes everything. Along with two humans, their names are the masculine and feminine form of the word Life or Life of the Body. It all begins new, the old wounds have been cauterized and the world enjoys a new hope. For those of us who find our way to Asatru it is important that we also find new hope, that we embrace a faith which encourages and supports life and supports the idea that no matter the struggle we have what it takes to make it through whatever is happening at the moment and try it again. It is when we find the courage to try it again, to hold on to our faith and finally discover we can do it that we earn the wisdom we are told about in these Eddas.

Made in the USA
Middletown, DE
08 July 2023

34738355R00086